THE STORY OF

Thomas Alva Edison

INVENTOR

The Wizard of Menlo Park

THE STORY OF

Thomas Alva Edison

INVENTOR

The Wizard of Menlo Park

by

MARGARET DAVIDSON

SCHOLASTIC INC.
New York Toronto London Auckland Sydney

ISBN 0-590-42403-3

Text copyright © 1964 by Margaret Davidson.

Illustrations copyright © 1990 by Scholastic Inc.

All rights reserved. Published by Scholastic Inc.

12 11 10 9 8 7 6 5 4 3 2 1   0 1 2 3 4 5/9

Printed in the U.S.A.   40

First Scholastic printing, March 1990

To Tom and Ruth

Contents

Once there was a boy who asked a lot of questions. His favorite word was *why*. Sometimes he got answers to his questions. And sometimes he did not. For sometimes people didn't want to bother with his questions.

His own father grew angry with him. One day he said, "Tom, all you are is one big question mark. I have a question mark for a son!"

But Tom didn't stop asking questions. He was curious about everything in his world.

Thomas Edison was born over one hundred years ago in the town of Milan, Ohio. He was born on February 11, 1847. At that

time, in all of America — in all of the world — there were no telephones, no automobiles, no movies, no radios.

In all of the world, there was not one electric light.

As soon as he could speak, Tom began to ask questions. Many times he was not happy with other people's answers. So when he grew up, Tom worked out his own answers. And the special answers of Thomas Alva Edison were inventions. One of his inventions was the phonograph. Another was motion pictures. And Tom's biggest invention of all pushed back the dark. It was the electric light.

TOM'S FIRST EXPERIMENT

When Tom was four years old, he noticed something odd in the barn. He noticed that the family goose sat on her eggs all the time.

"Why does our goose sit on the eggs, Mother?" Tom asked.

"Because she wants to keep them warm."

"But why?"

"Because they will hatch if they stay warm," his mother answered.

"But what does *hatch* mean?" Tom wanted to know.

"*Hatch* means coming out of an egg, Tom. It means being born, for a baby goose."

Mrs. Edison picked up an egg. "See how warm it is. When it is ready, a baby goose will come out of this shell." Then gently she put the egg back on the nest.

"The eggs have to be warm to hatch?"

"That's right, Tom."

Tom's family was worried. Hours had passed since they had seen him. It was night, and they couldn't find Tom. His father, his mother, and his older sister, Tannie, looked through the house for him. They looked in the yard. Then they looked in the barn — and found Tom curled up on the nest.

"What are you doing, Tom Edison?" his father roared. Tom had an answer ready. He was hatching eggs. He was making baby geese.

His sister Tannie burst out laughing. "You are the goose, Tom Edison," she said. "Just look at those eggs! Just look at your pants!"

Poor Tom. He was all egg.

Tom was only four. But he was much too heavy to sit on an egg. He was only four and very disappointed. He started to cry.

This was Tom Edison's first experiment. And it was a failure.

NO MORE SCHOOL

In 1854 the Edisons moved away from Milan. The family went by train to Detroit. There they got on a riverboat called the *Ruby*. And they went west on the St. Clair River until they came to Port Huron, Michigan. This was their new home.

Tom started school. The schoolmaster, Mr. Engle, had a terrible temper. He didn't like children very much. Most of all, he didn't like Tom Edison, who asked so many questions.

One day Mr. Engle lost his temper. "Tom Edison," he thundered, "all you do is ask silly questions. There is nothing I can do with you — your brains are addled!"

When Mrs. Edison heard what the schoolmaster said, she was angry. Addled! Weak in the head! Her son was not addled. But she could not say as much for Mr. Engle!

Mrs. Edison took Tom out of school. She would teach him herself. Tom never went back to school. In all his life, Thomas Edison spent only three months in school.

Tom Edison didn't go to school, but he was a great reader. He read all kinds of books. When Tom was nine, he read a science book. It told about chemicals and carbons and electricity. *Electricity.* How Tom loved that word. This book changed Tom's life. He decided to become an inventor.

TOM GOES TO WORK

Tom needed money for his experiments. He needed money for science books. So when Tom Edison was twelve years old, he went to work.

Tom had to leave his house in Port Huron every morning at seven o'clock. He didn't get home until long after dark. For Tom sold newspapers on a train — on the Detroit express. He also sold molasses candy and sandwiches. He walked through the cars calling, "Newspapers, apples, sandwiches, molasses, peanuts!"

Tom made money on the train. But he needed more money — more money for his experiments and his science books. What could he do to earn money? Tom thought about this for some time. Then he had an idea. He would put out his *own* newspaper. He would write it, and print it, and sell it.

But where could he work? There was plenty of room in the baggage car on the train. Tom bought an old printing press and put it in the baggage car. And he started to work — writing, printing, and selling copies of his own newspaper, *The Weekly Herald.*

Tom didn't spell very well. Sometimes he forgot to put periods at the end of his sentences. So they ran on and on and on. But people bought his newspaper. They liked the stories in *The Weekly Herald.* And Tom's spelling made them laugh.

Now Tom made more money. But he had one more problem. Tom had the money

for his experiments, but he didn't have time! All day long, and far into the night, Tom was on the train. He was very tired when he got home. He was too tired to do his experiments so late at night.

Tom thought of a way to solve this problem, too. He moved his glass jars and his chemicals. He moved his whole laboratory from his home into the baggage car! This was the first moving laboratory in the world.

An Accident!

Tom was always in a hurry. He had so many jobs to do. One morning, Tom was late. The train was pulling out of the station — and without him!

Tom ran very fast. He grabbed hold of the back of the train. But his arms were full of bundles. His fingers held on tightly, but those bundles got in the way!

The train clicked and clacked as it went faster and faster. The wheels clicked and clacked — as they waited to catch Tom's legs.

Tom was slipping! A man on the train saw him. The man came running through the car. He reached down and grabbed Tom. He grabbed the first thing he could get hold of. He grabbed Tom's ears. And the man pulled Tom up to safety.

Tom Edison felt something go "snap" inside his head. Very soon he was quite deaf. He could hear people shout. He could hear the roar of the train. He could hear if a person stood very close to him and yelled in his ear. But all the soft sounds of the world were lost to Tom Edison.

Tom tried not to mind. He taught himself to read other people's lips. He said the silence gave him room to think. But years later he wrote in his diary, "I haven't heard a bird sing since I was twelve years old."

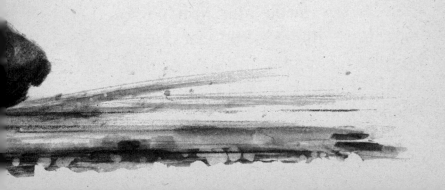

How Tom Became a Telegraph Operator

For three more years Tom worked on the train. By the summer of 1862, he was fifteen years old. Then one day the train pulled into the Mt. Clemens station. This was where his friend, Mr. Mackenzie, worked as a telegraph operator.

Tom hopped off quickly and ran into the telegraph office. He liked to watch Mr. Mackenzie work in the dusty office. Tom loved the mysterious machinery.

Tom looked through the window. And what he saw made him rush out of the office. Little Jimmie, Mr. Mackenzie's son, was playing on the tracks. A train was coming down those tracks — straight for Jimmie!

Tom took a flying leap — right in front of the train. He grabbed the little boy. And they rolled and tumbled to safety. Tom felt his heel bang against the side of the train. It was that close.

Mr. Mackenzie's voice shook. "What can I ever do to repay you, Tom?" Tom looked toward the telegraph office. Mr. Mackenzie understood. He would teach Tom the secrets of the telegraph.

Tom studied hard. Five months later, a proud boy shook hands with Mr. Mackenzie. Tom was only sixteen years old, but now he could do a man's job. Now he could join the men who wandered from town to town — men who called themselves telegraph operators.

For five years Tom wandered. From Ohio to Missouri and then to Alabama. From Mississippi to the Carolinas, and back to his home again. During these years of work, he did a lot of dreaming. Five exciting years — and ideas began to grow.

A Man's Job

When Tom was twenty-one years old, he went to New York City. He was a young man. The wandering years were over.

Now Tom wanted to invent all the ideas he had in his head. But he had no money. So Tom went to work for other men. He worked for men who owned big machines — new machines that ran by electricity. Sometimes a machine went too fast or too slow, or not at all. Tom was very good at inventing ways to make these machines better. And he began to make money.

On Christmas Day in 1871, Tom was married. Tom and his wife, Mary, had a little girl. Now Tom had a family. He was making more and more money. He had the respect of some important men in New York City. But he wasn't happy. Not at all. Tom didn't want to work for other men. He didn't want to make better and better machines for other men. He wanted to invent — all by himself.

THE INVENTION FACTORY

In 1876, Tom stopped working for other men. He bought a piece of land called Menlo Park, in New Jersey. On the land Tom built a plain wooden building. The first floor was for offices. The second floor was one big room. This was the room for making inventions. Tom built a white picket fence around the building — to keep the pigs and cows out. He called the building an *invention factory*.

At Menlo Park there were mechanics and glass blowers and builders. And one dreamer — Tom Edison.

In 1876, most of the world had never heard of Tom Edison. He was only twenty-nine years old. The men who knew him didn't think much of Tom's new ideas. These men thought he had big dreams. They laughed at him for building an invention factory.

They said to one another, "He's clever with his hands. He's clever at fixing our machines. He can take our machines and make them better. But he only went to school for three months! And now he wants to make his own machines. Now he wants to make his own inventions!"

Tom was very busy. And he had plans. He slept only four hours a day. The rest of the time he worked in his invention factory. Many times he locked himself in the big room on the second floor. He stayed there for days. He didn't even go home to eat. Mrs. Edison sent in food. When he was sleepy, Tom lay down on the floor for a ten-minute nap. Then up he'd jump — ready to work some more.

Once a friend tried to slow Tom down. But Tom said, "I have so much to do, and life is so short. I've got to hustle."

WOOD AND METAL TALK!

Tom drew a picture of his idea on a piece of paper. He nodded his head. Tom had been working on this idea for months. Now he was satisfied.

"John," he called. "Can you make this machine for me?" John Kreusi, one of Tom's workers, looked at the drawing. "Sure," John answered. "It's simple."

John went away and started to work. But he was puzzled. This was a strange machine. It had no wires. It had no motor. It had no electricity at all. It was round. It had a handle. It was made of wood and metal. It was a very simple machine. What could such a simple machine do?

John laid down his tools. He *had* to ask. "Mr. Edison, what is this machine for?"

Tom looked up from his book. "For? Why, this machine will talk," Tom said. Then he went back to reading his book.

John shook his head. Maybe the men in New York City were right to laugh at Tom Edison! His boss was smart — but a machine that talked! Wood and metal that talked! This was magic. No, John decided, his boss must be joking. Even Tom Edison couldn't make magic.

Soon all of Menlo Park knew of the machine — and what Tom said it would do. One man whispered to another. And then the second man whispered to a third. And they all shook their heads.

After thirty hours of work, John Kreusi came into Tom's office. He held the finished machine in his hands. All the men in the factory crowded around.

Tom bent over the machine. Very gently, he moved some of the parts. Then he started to speak into it:

"Mary had a little lamb,
Its fleece was white as snow,
And everywhere that Mary went
The lamb was sure to go."

The men looked at one another. What was he doing? Tom moved some of the parts again. And he started to turn the handle.

Sqwaaaaaaaaaaaaaaaaaaak!

That was all that came from the machine! The men turned away. They didn't want to see their boss look like a fool.

But Tom just bent over the machine again. He saw that a part had slipped. He put it back in place. And he started to speak again: "Mary had a little lamb. . . ." A second time he turned the handle.

For a moment the whole room was silent. Everyone held his breath. Then — clearly, plainly — out of the machine came the voice of Thomas Alva Edison:

"Mary had a little lamb. . . ."

Now the whole world knew about Thomas Edison. People called him a wizard — a magic maker. Soon, all over America, people were talking about him. They called him the Wizard of Menlo Park. For in the winter of 1877, Tom Edison made wood and metal talk. He invented the phonograph.

TOM'S ELECTRIC LIGHT

The Wizard was busy. He said he was too busy to pay attention to what people said about him. He had a new idea.

Tom looked at the candle on his desk. He looked at the fireplace. He looked at the oil lamp hanging in the window. The light from the candle was weak. The light from the fire was full of shadows. The oil lamp smelled.

So in 1878 Tom Edison began his greatest adventure. He tried to take electricity — and turn it into light.

Other inventors had worked on this problem. One kind of light, called a carbon arc light, had already been invented. It used electricity. But the carbon arc light wasn't what Tom had in mind at all. The arc light was very, very bright. It made a strange, loud noise — hizzzzuuuzzzzz. It went out often. When people stood near the arc light, they got dirty. The light smelled bad. It cost a lot of money. And it caused fires.

Tom wanted a very different light. He wanted to make a soft light. Tom wanted his light to shine with a steady glow. He wanted a light that had no smell, no noise, no danger. And most of all, Tom wanted a cheap light. He wanted to make a light that everyone could buy and put in their homes.

Other scientists didn't think Tom's idea would work. Nobody, they said — not even Tom Edison — could make a light that was steady, silent, safe, soft, clean, *and* cheap.

But Tom was very sure of himself. He

always was. This time, Tom bragged about his idea. He talked to a newspaper reporter from New York City. Tom told the reporter all about his dream. He said he would have the whole invention done in six weeks. Six weeks! Six weeks was a very short time to give his electric light to the world.

Tom went to work. Six weeks passed. Six months passed. And no light came from Menlo Park. Tom found out it wasn't so easy to make his idea work after all.

As the months passed, people stopped calling Tom the Wizard of Menlo Park. They called him *dreamer* and *fool* instead.

But Tom kept on. He had been wrong to tell people he would be done in six weeks. He had been wrong about that. But Tom knew he was right about his light. Anyway, Tom never bothered much about what other people thought.

Tom's light was inside a glass bulb. Inside the bulb Tom put a filament — a thin thread made of carbon. Tom wanted to make this filament very, very hot. He knew that very hot material gave off light. So Tom used electricity to heat the filament.

Tom wanted the filament to *glow with heat.* (When material glows with heat, it is called *incandescent.* Tom was trying to make the first incandescent electric light.)

First, Tom took two metal wires. He tied one end of each wire to the filament. He tied the other ends to a generator — a machine that makes electricity. When he turned on the generator, electricity came from it. The electricity traveled up the wire and inside the glass bulb. It ran into the filament. The filament got hot. It got so hot it turned white. It gave off light! But only for a moment. Then the filament got

too hot. It got so hot it burned up and turned dark again.

Tom thought something might be wrong with his filament material. Was there a better material for his thread of light? Tom tried rubber and cork filaments. He tried corn silk, metal, hemp, straw, silk, and splinters of wood. He even tried human hair. Nothing worked.

Tom was disappointed. But he was also stubborn. When Tom was disappointed, he sometimes said sharp things. This time he said, "I'll never quit until I get what I want! That's the difference between the other fellow and me. Sometimes they quit. I won't."

Tom continued to question. What made that filament burn up?

Tom made drawings in his notebook. He did more experiments. He thought about all the science facts he knew. Then one day Tom had an idea. "Yes, that's it," he said to himself. "We will pump the air out! We will take the air out of the bulb. It's

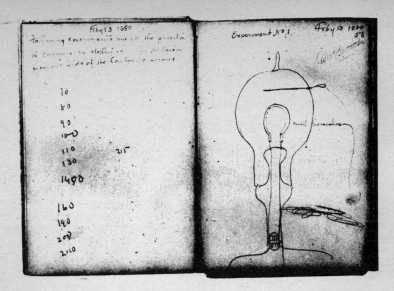

These are pages from Tom Edison's notebooks.

the air that's working against my light."
Tom knew that oxygen — a part of air —
helped make material burn.

His filament was burning up.

But if there wasn't any oxygen inside the
bulb . . . . If there wasn't any oxygen near
his filament . . . . Then the filament would
not burn up.

Now the light was better. It burned six
minutes. But it wasn't good enough. What
made it die?

Tom fussed. He worried. His idea for an
incandescent light was good. He knew it

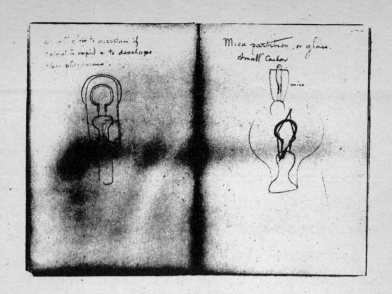

was. What was he doing wrong? After many more months of careful work, Tom thought he had the answer. He was leaving something undone.

Tom took another bulb. He put a filament inside it. He took two metal wires, and he tied one end of each wire to the filament. He tied the other end of the metal wires to the generator. Then he pumped the air out of the bulb.

This was just what he'd been doing for months. But this time he didn't turn on the electricity. This time he didn't send electricity into the filament. Not right away.

He sat back and waited a few minutes. Then he turned the pump back on. His helpers were puzzled. Why was Mr. Edison turning on the pump again? He had already taken the air out.

The men looked at the pump. More air was coming out of the bulb! Tom's helpers were amazed. Where had this extra air come from?

Tom explained. The air came from *inside the filament,* he said. It also came from inside the walls of the glass bulb. "Yes," Tom said. "This tiny bit of hidden air is what worked against my light."

Now Tom was sure his light would work. But he was very tired. He was so tired that he lay down on a bench for a ten-minute nap. Then he was up — and ready. It was eight o'clock at night, October 19, 1879.

Tom turned on the electricity. The filament heated up. It turned white. It gave off light. Tom sat back to watch. A minute passed. Then two. Then ten. And the light didn't die!

The bulb burned all night. It burned all the next day, and into the next. For more than forty hours, Tom's bulb shone with a clean, soft, steady light. The electric light was born.

Good-bye to Menlo Park

Four years later Tom's Menlo Park days
came to an end. In 1884 Tom's wife, Mary,
died. The little laboratory made him sad.
It reminded him of happier days. Tom
closed Menlo Park. He took his children
and moved to New York.

For two years Tom was very lonely. Then
one day a friend invited Tom to dinner.
At his friend's house, Tom met Mina Miller.
Mina made Tom very happy. But Tom was
too deaf to hear her voice. So Tom taught
Mina the Morse Code — the dot-dot-dash

language of the telegraph. They tapped talk
into each other's hands. They spoke to each
other by Morse Code.

One day Tom tapped a question into
Mina's hand. And she tapped back —
Y-E-S. Tom and Mina Miller were married
in 1886.

Tom was ready to go back to inventing. First he built a new invention factory. His new laboratory was in West Orange, New Jersey. And it was very big — much bigger than Menlo Park.

Tom's Menlo Park days were over. But he was only forty years old, and he had many more things to invent.

THE SECRET OF ROOM 5

Soon after Tom built the West Orange laboratory, he had another really big idea. He didn't let anybody know about it for a long time. It was a secret. Tom had learned a bitter lesson. He learned that talking about his ideas was not always smart. Sometimes people stole his ideas. They used his ideas to make inventions, and then said the inventions belonged to them.

So Tom kept his new invention a secret. Tom and his helpers worked on it behind a locked door. They called it "the secret of Room 5."

The men did experiment after experiment. They made model after model. Each model was better than the last one. But none was good enough. Then one day in the summer of 1889 Tom yelled, "We've got it! Now work!"

Tom knew the secret invention was ready to be born. He'd done his work. He would let his helpers build the final model. Tom wanted a rest. So the Edisons left for a vacation in Europe.

When Tom came back from his trip, his helpers met him. They took him to a room and told him to sit down. A big machine was in the back of the room. Next to the big machine was one of Tom's phonographs.

Suddenly the room was dark. A whirring sound filled the room. A light came from the strange machine. On the white wall facing Tom, a man appeared. The man bowed. A voice coming from the phonograph said, "Good morning, Mr. Edison.

Glad to see you back. I hope you are satisfied . . . ."

The wonderful secret of Room 5 was a movie. Tom had invented a kind of motion picture.

THE BIG FIRE

The years passed. Tom Edison kept on inventing. He was very rich, but he kept on hustling.

Then, on a cold December night in 1914, something happened that made Tom work harder than ever. His laboratory caught fire. The fire started in a small wooden storage building. In that building chemicals were stored. Green and yellow chemical flames spread to all the Edison buildings.

Tom stood watching. His son Charles tried to comfort him. Tom just said, "It's

all right. I am sixty-seven years old. But I'm not too old to make a fresh start."

And he did. In a few weeks Tom Edison was back at work again. The years went by. They were busy years. Tom went on inventing.

THE END

Now Tom was eighty-four years old. He had lived a long life. It was almost over. All through his life he faced the unknown and made it known. A few weeks before his death, Tom said to his wife, Mina, "I've lived my life. I've done my work."

Everyone was sad that Tom Edison was dying. All over America people followed the news about his illness.

The newspaper reporters didn't want to bother Mrs. Edison. They waited each day and every night in the yard under Tom's bedroom window. Mrs. Edison promised to tell the reporters when the end came.

She would give them a signal. The signal would be this: When the time came, she would turn off the light that burned in Tom's room.

Early in the morning of October 18, 1931, the light Tom invented went off in his bedroom. The Wizard of Menlo Park was dead.

There is no Menlo Park today. After Tom and his family left in 1884, it stood empty for years. Then a farmer moved in and raised pigs in the long laboratory building. It began to fall apart. One day, the building caught on fire and burned to the ground.

But you can see Edison's inventions today. The many inventions of Thomas Alva Edison are at the laboratory in West Orange, New Jersey. Five buildings have been turned into a museum.

You can see and touch his electric light, his movie camera, his phonograph, and his many other inventions.

You can see the goldenrod plant. Edison invented a way to make rubber from this wild plant.

You can see Edison's storage battery and a model of his electric train. The books Tom Edison read are there. And so are the 3,400 notebooks he filled with notes and drawings for his experiments. The walls of the museum are covered with pictures of Edison at work.

You can see his laboratory coat. It is hanging on a wall peg — right where he put it after his last day of work in 1931.

Almost everything Thomas Edison wrote about or made is there. Some day you may be able to visit the museum. Write for information to:

Thomas A. Edison National Historic Site
Main Street and Lakeside Avenue
West Orange, New Jersey
07052

Thomas Alva Edison's inventions were beginnings. They have been improved. They have been changed. Would Tom Edison recognize some of his own inventions today?

This is a picture of the first incandescent electric light.

Today we have many kinds of light bulbs for many different jobs. They all began with that first electric light.

Tom's first movie camera was a very heavy machine.

Today cameras are so light that you can carry many of them.

The first phonograph records
were shaped like a piece of
lead pipe or a rolling pin.

Later Tom improved the phonograph
machine. He put a big horn on it.
This made it sound better.
He also made a better record.
It was flat, just as the ones of
today are.

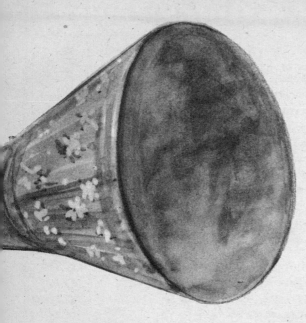

Today there are compact
disc players that use
lasers to produce sound.

Step Back in Time with
SCHOLASTIC BIOGRAPHY

☐ MP41836-X	Custer and Crazy Horse: A Story of Two Warriors	$2.75
☐ MP42969-8	The Death of Lincoln: A Picture History of the Assassination	$2.75
☐ MP40512-8	The Defenders	$2.50
☐ MP43733-X	The First Woman Doctor	$2.75
☐ MP42218-9	Frederick Douglass Fights for Freedom	$2.50
☐ MP43628-7	Freedom Train: The Story of Harriet Tubman	$2.75
☐ MP41024-5	Great Escapes of World War II	$2.50
☐ MP42402-5	Harry Houdini: Master of Magic	$2.50
☐ MP42404-1	Helen Keller	$2.50
☐ MP42395-9	Jesse Jackson: A Biography	$2.75
☐ MP43503-5	Jim Abbott: Against All Odds	$2.75
☐ MP41344-9	John Fitzgerald Kennedy: America's 35th President	$2.50
☐ MP41159-4	Lost Star: The Story of Amelia Earhart	$2.75
☐ MP42659-1	Mr. President: A Book of U.S. Presidents	$2.75
☐ MP42644-3	Our 41st President George Bush	$2.50
☐ MP43481-0	Pocahontas and the Strangers	$2.75
☐ MP41877-7	Ready, Aim, Fire! The Real Adventures of Annie Oakley	$2.75
☐ MP41183-7	Secret Missions: Four True-Life Stories	$2.50
☐ MP43052-1	The Secret Soldier	$2.50
☐ MP42560-9	Stealing Home: A Story of Jackie Robinson	$2.75
☐ MP42403-3	The Story of Thomas Alva Edison, Inventor	$2.50
☐ MP41342-2	They Led the Way: 14 American Women	$2.50
☐ MP40488-1	The Wright Brothers at Kitty Hawk	$2.50

Available wherever you buy books, or use the coupon below.